ARE YOU S[...]
THAN A 5 [...]

D0395941

TEST YOUR SMARTS!

by Kris Hirschmann
and Ryan Herndon

Thanks to Mark Burnett Productions,
especially Mark Burnett, Barry Poznick, John Stevens,
Sue Guercioni, Amanda Harrell, and Laura Ambriz

SCHOLASTIC INC.
New York Toronto London Auckland Sydney
Mexico City New Delhi Hong Kong Buenos Aires

■ SCHOLASTIC

Are You
Smarter Than
a 5th Grader

The publisher would like to thank the following for their kind permission to use their photographs in this book: 5 Washington Monument © Gary Blakeley/Shutterstock; 6 Soldier © Lvector/Shutterstock; 9 Everglades National Park © chloé beaufreton/istockphoto.com; 10 George Washington, 67 Abraham Lincoln © pandapaw/Shutterstock; 11 Continent map © zabi/Shutterstock; 12 Compass rose © Dawid Krupa/Shutterstock, Globe © samara/Shutterstock; 14 Statue of Liberty © Albo/Shutterstock; 15, 45, 61, 77 Pencil © Stetom/Shutterstock; 15, 29 Eraser © Mariano N. Ruiz/Shutterstock; 20 Coins © Shebeko/Shutterstock; 22 Alamo © Sally Scott/Shutterstock; 25 Rain forest © STILLFX/Shutterstock; 26 Totem pole © Richard Welter/Shutterstock; 28 Pharaoh, 43 Ra Hieroglyph © Maugli/Shutterstock; 28 Parthenon © Brent Wong/Shutterstock; 31, 45, 61, 77 Pencil Sharpener © SNR/Shutterstock; 33 Gavel © Junial Enterprises/Shutterstock; 34 White House © Albert de Bruijn/Shutterstock; 35 Nebraska © Steven Bourelle/Shutterstock; 36 Sierra Nevada © Zack Frank/Shutterstock; 37 Dogsled © iztok noc/istockphoto.com; 38 Alps © Carsten Madsen/istockphoto.com; 39 Penguin art © Hano Uzeirbegovic/Shutterstock; 41 Telephone © Marc Dietrich/Shutterstock; 44 Great Wall © Mikhail Nekrasov/Shutterstock; 50 Penny © Mario Bruno/Shutterstock; 51 American Flag © Brandon Seidel/Shutterstock; 54 Everest sign © Stuart Murchison/istockphoto.com; 55 Desert © Sean Randall/istockphoto.com; 56 Coliseum © S. Greg Panosian/istockphoto.com; 57 Native American Chief art © Jeremy Mayes/istockphoto.com; 59 Japanese plane © Dennys Bisogno/istockphoto.com; 60 Amelia Earhart, 76 Charles Lindbergh © AP Photo; 65 Capital Hill © Elena Yakusheva/Shutterstock; 66 People © Kirsty Pargeter/Shutterstock; 69 Podium © Dieter Spears/istockphoto.com; 71 Gobi Desert © David Ciemny/istockphoto.com; 72 Supreme Court © Jason Maehl/Shuttterstock; 74 Gold panning © Robert Gubbins/istockphoto.com; 75 Queen Hieroglyph © Harald Bolten/istockphoto.com; 80 Mortarboard art © Dr. Flash/Shutterstock.

ISBN-13: 978-0-545-12042-5
ISBN-10: 0-545-12042-X

Designed by Michelle Martinez
Photo researched by Michelle Martinez, Debra Cohn-Orbach, and Els Rijper

12 11 10 9 8 7 6 5 4 3 2 1   9 10 11 12 13 14/0

Printed in the U.S.A.
First printing, March 2009

HISTORY

SMARTY ALERT

Lights . . . Camera . . . ACTION!
Since its debut in 2007, the hit game show
"Are You Smarter Than A 5th Grader?" has
proven that most adults *did* forget their
grade-school lessons. During the show's first
two seasons, not one contestant has taken
home the $1,000,000 grand prize.

Think you can do better? Here's your chance
to test your smarts in the subject of
HISTORY. Will you ace this test or flunk
out? Grab a pencil, turn the page, and find
out if you're smarter than a 5th grader!

1ST Grade

HISTORIC BEGINNINGS

Think back to first grade. That was the year you may have memorized the nation's presidents, its 50 states, and founding history. Basic facts every American knows, right? On the TV show, and sometimes in real life, even a smart person is stumped by the most basic questions. Do you remember your first-grade lessons . . . or is it ancient history?

1. What is the title of the U.S. national anthem?

2. How many stars appear on the U.S. flag?
   a) 40
   b) 50
   c) 60

3. In what month do we observe Columbus Day?

4. What is the name of the pictured landmark, which is located in our nation's capital?

5. According to the U.S. Constitution, what elected official in the executive branch of the government is commander-in-chief of the United States Army?

6. In the U.S., which is the title for the official elected to run a state?
   a) Mayor
   b) Governor
   c) Senator

7. Which of the following is a U.S. federal holiday?
   a) Arbor Day
   b) Flag Day
   c) New Year's Day

8. Which U.S. federal holiday honors men and women who have died in military service?
   a) Flag Day
   b) Veterans Day
   c) Memorial Day

9. The month of November has how many federal holidays?

10. Irving Berlin wrote what patriotic anthem that contains the words, "Stand beside her and guide her"?

U.S. PRESIDENTS

11. Who was the 16th President of the United States?

12. **True or False?** The White House is the official residence of both the U.S. President and Vice President.

13. What was the first name of the first U.S. First Lady?

AaBbCcDdEe

U.S. GEOGRAPHY

14. What is the capital of the United States of America?

15. If you cross the northern border of the U.S., what country are you in?

16. In terms of land area, what is the smallest state?

17. What is the largest state?

18. **True or False?** Including Alaska and Hawaii, there are more U.S. states that border the Pacific Ocean than the Atlantic Ocean.

19. Alana went on a trip to see Everglades National Park. What state did she go to?

20. What state borders South Dakota to the north?

21. The state of Indiana borders which Great Lake?

22. Which ocean borders the state of Georgia?

23. What state is nicknamed the Lone Star State?

24. How many U.S. states do not border another state?

25. What word does the "C" stand for in the U.S. city known as Washington D.C.?

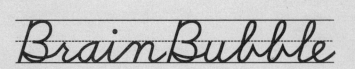

Brain Bubble

On Its Own

Washington, D.C. is not a part of any U.S. state. It is a federal district that was created for the sole purpose of housing the U.S. government. It was established on July 16, 1790, by a Congressional act known as the Residence Act. The city was named in honor of George Washington, the first U.S. President.

WORLD GEOGRAPHY

26. What is the only continent that is also a country?

27. What continent lies directly east of Europe?

28. More than 95% of which continent is covered by an ice sheet?

29. What continent is highlighted on this map of the world?

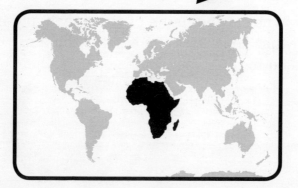

30. India borders which ocean?

31. Which of the world's oceans lies directly north of Asia?

32. How many continents share a land border with Antarctica?

33. On this compass rose, the top arrow indicates which cardinal direction?

34. What is the name of the imaginary line that separates the earth's top and bottom halves?

35. This map shows which water features?

a) Lakes
b) Rivers
c) Oceans

36. What is the name of a round object printed or painted to look like the Earth?

37. The United States is located on what continent?

U.S. HISTORY

38. Which of these American heroes is fictional?
a) Johnny Appleseed
b) Paul Bunyan
c) Davy Crockett

39. Which ocean did Christopher Columbus cross when he traveled from Europe to the New World?
a) Atlantic Ocean
b) Pacific Ocean
c) Indian Ocean

40. **True or False?** The Statue of Liberty was a gift to the United States from Italy.

Brain Bubble

Lady Liberty

The Statue of Liberty is sometimes nicknamed "Lady Liberty." Its official name, however, is "Liberty Enlightening the World." Built of steel-reinforced copper, the statue is more than 151 feet tall, and stands on a pedestal of about the same height. It sits on Liberty Island in New York Harbor, looking out toward the ocean.

7x7=49 AaBbCcDdEe

Brain Benders

41. What modern holiday is also known as "All Hallow's Eve"?

42. True or False? The year 1895 was in the 19th century.

SOCIAL STUDIES

1. **"The Star-Spangled Banner."** The song's lyrics come from a poem written in 1814 by Francis Scott Key.

2. **b. 50**. The U.S. flag bears one star for each of our nation's 50 states.

3. **October**. Columbus Day is celebrated on the second Monday of this month each year.

4. **The Washington Monument**. It was completed and dedicated in 1885.

5. **The U.S. President**. He or she has overall authority of all U.S. defensive forces.

6. **b. Governor**. Mayors run cities. Senators are Congressional officials.

7. **c. New Year's Day**. Arbor Day and Flag Day are unofficial celebrations.

8. **c. Memorial Day**. This holiday is observed each year on the last Monday of May.

9. **Two**. Veterans Day is observed on November 11. Thanksgiving is observed on the fourth Thursday of the month.

10. **"God Bless America."** This well-known song was written in 1918.

U.S. PRESIDENTS

11. **Abraham Lincoln**. He was President from March 4, 1861 to April 15, 1865.

12. **False**. Only the President and his or her family live in the White House.

13. **Martha**. She was the wife of George Washington, the first U.S. President.

U.S. GEOGRAPHY

14. **Washington, D.C.**

15. **Canada**. This nation shares a long border with the United States.

16. **Rhode Island**. This state is only about 37 miles wide and 48 miles long.

17. **Alaska**. The state of Rhode Island could fit into Alaska 425 times.

18. **False**. Just five U.S. states border the Pacific. Not including the Gulf of Mexico, 14 states border the Atlantic Ocean.

19. **Florida**. The Everglades are found at the southern tip of this peninsula state.

20. **North Dakota**. This state lies between South Dakota and Canada.

21. **Lake Michigan**. The lake touches Indiana's northwestern edge.

34. **The Equator**. This line marks the middle point of our planet.

35. a. **Lakes**. A large body of water completely surrounded by land is a lake.

36. **A globe**. It shows our planet in its actual form instead of laid out flat, as on paper maps.

37. **North America**. This continent also includes Canada, Greenland, Mexico, and some island nations.

U.S. HISTORY
38. b. **Paul Bunyan**. This fictional lumberjack appeared in stories in the early 1900s. Johnny Appleseed and Davy Crockett were both real people.

39. a. **Atlantic Ocean**. This ocean separates the continents of Europe and North America.

40. **False**. The Statue of Liberty was a gift from France. It arrived in the United States in 1886.

BRAIN BENDERS
41. **Halloween**. This holiday is celebrated on October 31 each year.

42. **True**. The 19th century ran from January 1, 1801 to December 31, 1900.

22. **The Atlantic Ocean**. The state's coastline is more than 100 miles long.

23. **Texas**. The Lone Star appears on the state's flag and official seal.

24. **Two**. Hawaii and Alaska are separated from the other 48 states.

25. **Columbia**. D.C. stands for "District of Columbia."

WORLD GEOGRAPHY
26. **Australia**. The Commonwealth of Australia is the only country on this island continent.

27. **Asia**. Asia and Europe are separated by convention only, not by any distinct geographic features.

28. **Antarctica**. This region makes up the Earth's southernmost continent.

29. **Africa**. It is the world's second largest and second most populous continent.

30. **The Indian Ocean**. This ocean lies directly to the south of India.

31. **The Arctic Ocean**. The world's smallest ocean lies north of Asia, Europe, and North America.

32. **Zero**. Antarctica is an island continent.

33. **North**. On traditional U.S. maps, "up" is always north.

Did you
☐ pass or
☐ fail?

2ND Grade

REDO OR REVIEW

Welcome to second grade! Everything seems familiar, like you've studied these subjects before. But now you'll find the lessons are longer and the questions are tougher . . . and you're smarter! Will this time around be a review of the lessons you learned, or a redo of the ones that tripped you up?

SOCIAL STUDIES

1. What's the minimum number of U.S. coins you need to make exactly 61 cents?

2. Who was the first woman to appear on American money?
   a) Sacagawea
   b) Betsy Ross
   c) Susan B. Anthony

3. In 1782, what became the official bird of the United States?

4. What U.S. city is known as the City of Brotherly Love?

5. In the patriotic song "America," what four words follow the lyrics, "My country 'tis of thee"?

6. What three words begin the Preamble to the U.S. Constitution?

7. What building is on the back of the U.S. $20 bill?

U.S. PRESIDENTS

8. **True or False?** The U.S. President must be a natural-born citizen of the United States.

9. In what year did construction begin on the White House?
   a) 1642
   b) 1792
   c) 1801

10. Which U.S. President is featured on the face of the nickel?

11. Where is the Lincoln Home National Historic Site located?

12. What state extends the farthest west?
    a) Alaska
    b) California
    c) Nevada

13. Which of the following states extends the farthest south?
    a) Utah
    b) New Mexico
    c) Nebraska

14. What state borders both Kansas and Utah?

AaBbCcDdEe

15. How many states have the word North, South, East, or West in their names?

16. Yosemite National Park is located in what state?

17. The Alamo, site of a famous siege in 1836, is located in what city?

18. Lake Superior borders how many states?

19. The majority of the state of Nevada is located in what time zone?

AaBbCcDdEe

7x7=49

20. Omaha is the most populous city in what state?

21. The active volcano Mount St. Helens is in what state?

22. Mount McKinley, the highest peak in North America, is in what state?

Brain Bubble

High Hills

Where does North America rank on a list of the world's highest peaks? Check it out in this chart.

Mountain	Continent	Peak (feet)
Mount Everest	Asia	29,035
Aconcagua	S. America	22,831
Mount McKinley	N. America	20,320
Mount Kilimanjaro	Africa	19,340
Mount Elbrus	Europe	18,481
Puncak Jaya	Oceania	16,503
Vinson Massif	Antarctica	16,066

WORLD GEOGRAPHY

23. After China, what country on Earth has the biggest population?

24. France borders which ocean?

25. What is the capital of Spain?

26. The Caribbean Sea is part of which ocean?

27. The Earth's largest rain forest is located on what continent?

28. The majority of the International Date Line is in the middle of what ocean?

29. The country of Chile is located on which continent?

30. Which of the seven continents is the smallest in area?

31. The Equator crosses which three continents?

AaBbCcDdEe

U.S. HISTORY

32. The Liberty Bell is famous for what flaw?
a) A dent
b) A missing clapper
c) A crack

33. **True or False?** The colonial towns of Plymouth and Jamestown were both located in the colony of Virginia.

34. What is the name of this traditional object, carved from wood by Native Americans of the U.S. Pacific Northwest?

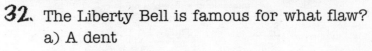

AaBbCcDdEe

7x7=49

35. Name the New York facility that was the main point of entry for U.S. immigrants from 1892 to 1954.

36. In the mid-1800s, the first transcontinental railway was built across part of the United States. One end of the railway was in California. The other end was in what state?
a) Nebraska
b) Utah
c) Ohio

BrainBubble

The Golden Spike

Two different teams built the transcontinental railroad at the same time. One team started in the west, and the other team started in the east. The teams worked toward each other until they met in Promontory, Utah. On May 10, 1869, the two railway lines were connected with a golden spike, officially completing the first (but far from the last) east/west transportation line in the United States.

WORLD HISTORY

37. Egyptian pharaoh
Tutankhamen lived
approximately when?
a) 1400 CE
b) 1400 BCE
c) 500 CE

38. The Parthenon was built in what
ancient Greek city?

39. Name the ship the Pilgrims sailed from
Plymouth, England, to the Plymouth
Colony in America.

Brain Benders

EXTRA CREDIT

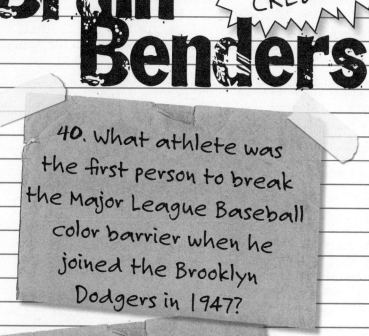

40. What athlete was the first person to break the Major League Baseball color barrier when he joined the Brooklyn Dodgers in 1947?

41. True or False? Civil rights activist Dr. Martin Luther King, Jr., was a medical doctor.

2ND GRADE ANSWER KEY

SOCIAL STUDIES

1. **Three**. A half dollar, a dime, and a penny total 61 cents.

2. **c. Susan B. Anthony**. A dollar coin bearing this voting-rights-activist's image was minted in 1979, 1980, 1981, and 1999.

3. **The bald eagle**. This bird was seen as a symbol of strength and liberty.

4. **Philadelphia, Pennsylvania**. The word "Philadelphia" comes from Greek words meaning City of Brotherly Love.

5. **"Sweet land of liberty."** Samuel Francis Smith wrote these lyrics in 1831.

6. **"We the people."** These three words are written in much larger letters than the rest of the document.

7. **The White House**. The front of the bill shows a portrait of U.S. President Andrew Jackson.

U.S. PRESIDENTS

8. **True**. To become President, a person must be American from birth.

9. **b. 1792**. Construction began October 13, 1792. John Adams and his family moved into the still-under-construction White House in 1800.

10. **Thomas Jefferson**. His profile has appeared on the nickel since 1938.

11. **Springfield, Illinois**. This site preserves the home Abraham Lincoln lived in before he became U.S. President.

U.S. GEOGRAPHY

12. **a. Alaska**. The entire state of Alaska lies west of the continental United States.

13. **b. New Mexico**. This state lies along the southernmost border of the United States.

14. **Colorado**. Kansas borders this state to the east. Utah borders it to the west.

15. **Five**. The states are North Carolina, North Dakota, South Carolina, South Dakota, and West Virginia.

16. **California**. The 1,189-square-mile park is found in the center of the state.

17. **San Antonio, Texas**. This former mission and fortress is now a museum.

18. **Three**. The states are Minnesota, Wisconsin, and Michigan.

19. **Pacific**. The town of West Wendover, Nevada, is the only part of the state officially on Mountain Time.

20. **Nebraska**. According to the 2000 U.S. Census, Omaha had 390,007 residents.

21. **Washington**. The volcano is best known for a catastrophic eruption in 1980.

30

22. **Alaska**. This mountain is also known as Denali. Mount McKinley rises 20,320 feet above sea level.

WORLD GEOGRAPHY

23. **India**. In 2008, this country had an estimated population of over 1.1 billion people.

24. **The Atlantic Ocean**. France also borders the Mediterranean Sea, which is considered part of the Atlantic system.

25. **Madrid**. More than 5 million people live in and immediately around this city.

26. **The Atlantic Ocean**. This body of water is located southeast of the Gulf of Mexico.

27. **South America**. The Amazon rain forest covers about 1.4 billion acres of land in nine nations.

28. **The Pacific Ocean**. For the most part, the International Date Line follows the meridian of 180 degrees longitude.

29. **South America**. Long and thin, Chile extends down much of the continent's western edge.

30. **Australia**. It is slightly smaller than Europe, the second-smallest continent.

31. **South America, Africa, and Asia**.

U.S. HISTORY

32. **c. A crack**. The famous bell cracked and was repaired several times before being declared unusable.

33. **False**. Plymouth was located in Massachusetts. Jamestown was in Virginia.

34. **Totem pole**. Many different tribes created and displayed totem poles.

35. **Ellis Island**. Today, Ellis Island remains open as a historical site and tourist attraction.

36. **a. Nebraska**. The railway ran from Sacramento, California, to Omaha, Nebraska.

WORLD HISTORY

37. **b. 1400 BCE**. "King Tut" ruled during the Egyptian period known as the New Kingdom.

38. **Athens**. Built in the 5th century BCE, this landmark still stands today.

39. **The Mayflower**. This ship made its famous journey in 1620.

BRAIN BENDERS

40. **Jackie Robinson**. His career signaled the end of segregation in American baseball.

41. **False**. Dr. Martin Luther King, Jr., was a minister. He held a Ph.D. in theology from Boston University.

Did you
☐ pass or
☐ fail?

3RD Grade

DIGGING DEEPER

Pick up that shovel and get ready to dig in. Third grade is the midway point on your journey from first to fifth grade. Your teachers want you to dig deeper into the history of the world, unearthing the reasons beneath the achievements. Will you discover buried treasure in the scholarly archives, or will an avalanche of facts overwhelm you?

SOCIAL STUDIES

1. An amendment to the U.S. Constitution must be ratified by what fraction of the states?
   a) Two-thirds
   b) Three-quarters
   c) All

2. How many justices serve on the U.S. Supreme Court?

3. The United Nations headquarters is in what city?

4. Which amendment to the U.S. Constitution gives us freedom of religion?

5. The U.S. Declaration of Independence was written and signed in what year?

U.S. PRESIDENTS

6. Which of the following people was a U.S. President?
a) Johns Hopkins
b) Franklin Pierce
c) Brigham Young

7. Which of the following positions is NOT a member of the U.S. Presidential Cabinet?
a) Secretary of Education
b) Attorney General
c) White House Press Secretary

8. What is the capital of Massachusetts?

9. This is an outline of what state?

10. What state's nickname is the Show Me State?

11. What state was named after a King of England?

12. What river forms the boundary between Indiana and Kentucky?

13. Helena is the capital of what state?

AaBbCcDdEe

14. What is the capital of Michigan?

15. What is the capital of Arkansas?

16. The Sierra Nevada mountain range in North America runs along the eastern edge of what state?

17. True or False? The Hawaiian Islands were once known as the Sandwich Islands.

18. The Four Corners is the only place in America where four states meet at one point. Colorado, Arizona, and New Mexico are three of the states. What is the fourth?

7x7=49   AaBbccDdEe

WORLD GEOGRAPHY

19. **True or False?** North America is in the Eastern hemisphere.

20. What ocean covers the North Pole?

21. What is the world's longest river?

22. **True or False?** The Equator passes through the southern tip of North America.

AaBbCcDdEe

23. The Equator intersects what other imaginary line at 0 degrees latitude, 0 degrees longitude?

24. What is the capital of the United Kingdom?

25. The Alps are a mountain range located primarily on which continent?

26. The Ganges River flows through Bangladesh and what other country?

7x7=49   AaBbcCDdEe

27. Which of these is not an independent country?
a) Greenland
b) Iceland
c) Sri Lanka

28. The South Pole is located on what continent?

U.S. HISTORY

29. In what state was the U.S. Civil War's Battle of Gettysburg fought?

30. **True or False?** Vermont was one of the original 13 colonies.

31. What American scientist is credited with inventing bifocals?

32. **True or False?** Paul Revere, famous for his midnight ride on horseback, also participated in the Boston Tea Party.

33. **True or False?** There were six major Native American tribes living in the area that is now the U.S. when Europeans first arrived in the New World.

34. **True or False?** Spanish colonies existed in the area that is now California long before European settlers arrived on America's East Coast.

35. In 1860-186, eleven Southern states seceded from the United States. They formed a group called what?

36. About how many years did the U.S. Civil War last?
a) Two years
b) Four years
c) Six years

37. **True or False?** Inventor Samuel Morse earned the nick-name "The Great Communicator" after he invented both the telegraph and the telephone.

WORLD HISTORY

38. **True or False?** Vikings, also known as Norsemen, originated in Scandinavia.

39. **True or False?** In ancient Egypt, mummification was considered a punishment. It was done to shame the families of dead criminals.

Brain Bubble

I Want My Mummy!

When mummification techniques were first invented, only dead kings received the privilege of this treatment. Later, the Egyptians started to mummify the kings' servants and even their pets. All of the mummies were entombed together along with the furniture, tools, games, and other goods they were thought to need in the afterlife.

7x7=49

40. What was the name for the Egyptian god of the sun?
a) Ra
b) Hathor
c) Ramses

41. In ancient Greece, how often were the Olympic games held?
a) Every year
b) Every four years
c) Every ten years

42. What was the primary language spoken in ancient Rome?
a) Latin
b) Italian
c) Greek

AaBbCcDdEe

43. Napoleon was the Emperor of France from 1804 to 1815. Was Napoleon his first name or his last name?

44. **True or False?** Explorer Christopher Columbus, who crossed the Atlantic in 1492, was born in Spain.

45. Around 221 BCE, a ruler named Qin Shi Huangdi ordered a wall to be built across northern China. What is the name of this wall?

AaBbccDdEe

7x7=49

Brain Benders

46. A pharaoh was the ruler of what ancient civilization?

47. True or False? Florence Nightingale, a pioneer of modern nursing, was born in Florence, Italy.

SOCIAL STUDIES

1. **b. Three-quarters**. This means at least 38 states must agree to the proposed amendment.

2. **Nine**. The slate consists of the U.S. Chief Justice and eight Associate Justices.

3. **New York City**. Although the building is in New York, the land it occupies is considered international territory.

4. **The First Amendment**. This amendment also addresses freedom of speech, freedom of the press, and freedom of assembly.

5. **1776**. This famous document was adopted on July 4, 1776.

U.S. PRESIDENTS

6. **b. Franklin Pierce**. He served as President from 1853 to 1857.

7. **c. White House Press Secretary**. The Press Secretary ranks one level below Cabinet members.

U.S. GEOGRAPHY

8. **Boston**. Besides being the state capital, Boston is the largest city in New England.

9. **Nebraska**. This state is located in the U.S. Midwest.

10. **Missouri**. The nickname is not official. It does, however, appear on Missouri license plates.

11. **Georgia**. In 1733, the state (then a colony) was named in honor of King George II.

12. **The Ohio River**. Indiana lies north of the river, and Kentucky lies south.

13. **Montana**. Less than 26,000 people make their homes in Helena.

14. **Lansing**. It is Michigan's sixth largest city.

15. **Little Rock**. The city gets its name from a rock formation on the Arkansas River.

16. **California**. Part of the range also lies in the state of Nevada.

17. **True**. Captain James Cook gave the islands this name in 1778. The name eventually fell into disuse.

18. **Utah**. This state's southeastern tip touches the other three states.

WORLD GEOGRAPHY

19. **False**. North America is in the Western hemisphere.

20. **The Arctic Ocean**. Ice covers much of this ocean's surface year-round.

21. **The Nile**. This mighty river is more than 4,000 miles long.

22. **False**. All of North America lies above the Equator.

23. **The Prime Meridian**. These lines intersect in the Atlantic Ocean somewhere south of Ghana and west of Gabon.

24. **London**. This city is also the capital of England.

25. **Europe**. The Alps run through Austria, France, Germany, Italy, Switzerland, and a few other European countries.

26. **India**. The Ganges River passes through northern India before reaching Bangladesh.

27. **a. Greenland**. It is a Danish province.

28. **Antarctica**. The South Pole is the Earth's southernmost point.

U.S. HISTORY
29. **Pennsylvania**. This famous battle took place from July 1 through July 3, 1863.

30. **False**. Vermont was never a colony. It was an independent state.

31. **Benjamin Franklin**. This influential thinker invented many useful items during his lifetime (1706-1790).

32. **True**. On December 16, 1773, Paul Revere helped dump British tea into Boston Harbor.

33. **False**. There were dozens of major tribes and many more minor ones.

34. **False**. Europeans first settled the East Coast in 1620. California's first Spanish settlement, San Diego, was founded in 1769.

35. **The Confederate States of America**. This group was also called the Confederacy.

36. **b. Four years**. The U.S. Civil War began in 1861 and ended in 1865.

37. **False**. Samuel Morse never had such a nickname. He did invent the telegraph, but the telephone was credited to inventor Alexander Graham Bell.

WORLD HISTORY
38. **True**. Vikings terrorized northern Europe from about the year 790 to 1066.

39. **False**. Mummification was the highest form of respect. It was done to preserve the body for the afterlife.

40. **a. Ra**. This god was also known as Amun-Ra.

41. **b. Every four years**. This tradition continues today.

42. **a. Latin**. Over centuries, Latin evolved into the Italian language spoken today.

43. **First name**. Napoleon's last name was Bonaparte.

44. **False**. Columbus was born in Genoa, Italy.

45. **The Great Wall of China**. The finished wall was more than 1,500 miles long.

BRAIN BENDERS
46. **Egypt**. All Egyptian kings are called by this title.

47. **True**. She was named after her place of birth.

Did you
☐ pass or
☐ fail?

4TH Grade

BRIDGING THE GAP

Stretch across the divide between third and fifth grades and where are you? Bridging the gap known as fourth grade! You can draw conclusions, make connections between facts and outcomes, and think for yourself. That's exactly when your teachers throw the major historic challenges at you. Here's your chance to prove that you can jump up to the next level!

SOCIAL STUDIES

1. According to Article 1 of the U.S. Constitution, what government official in the executive branch also serves as President of the U.S. Senate?

2. How long is one regular term for a U.S. Senator?

3. An American citizen must be at least how old to serve as a Congressperson in the U.S. House of Representatives?

4. **True or False?** Children born on U.S. soil to foreign parents automatically become U.S. citizens.

5. Passed on August 26, 1920, the 19th Amendment to the U.S. Constitution guaranteed what right to women?

6. Each U.S. penny bears an image of which U.S. President?

U.S PRESIDENTS

7. Since the late 1930s, what calendar date has been designated for the inauguration of a United States President?

8. According to the U.S. Constitution, what is the maximum number of consecutive years a person can serve as U.S. President?

9. Who was the first U.S. President to be impeached?

10. In what year was Abraham Lincoln first elected U.S. President?

11. What is the most common first name among U.S. Presidents?

12. What is the first name of former U.S. President Taylor?

13. In 1917, the U.S. entered World War One under which President?

14. Who was U.S. President immediately before Franklin Delano Roosevelt?

15. Before he eventually became President of the United States, Harry Truman was a Senator representing what state?

16. U.S. President Hayes was elected into office in 1876. What was his full name?

AaBbCcDdEe

17. Mount Vernon was the traditional family home of which U.S. President?

U.S. GEOGRAPHY

18. Two U.S. rivers are more than 2,000 miles long. One is the Mississippi. What is the other?

19. The headwaters of the Mississippi River are in what state?

20. Which of the following regions is a U.S. territory?
a) Puerto Rico
b) Bermuda
c) Aruba

21. How many states are located north of the Tropic of Cancer?

7x7=49   AaBbCcDdEe

22. The names of how many states begin with the letter "O"?

23. What is the southernmost state?

24. The Grand Canyon is found in what state?

Brain Bubble

Truly Grand

The Grand Canyon is considered one of the natural wonders of the world. Carved out of solid rock by the Colorado River, this gorge is about 1 mile deep, 4 to 18 miles wide, and 277 miles long. The most spectacular part of the canyon is protected as part of the Grand Canyon National Park, which was established in 1919. Today, this park attracts more than 4 million visitors each year.

WORLD GEOGRAPHY

25. Berne is the capital of what European country?

26. Mount Kilimanjaro is located on what continent?

27. What country borders Spain to the west?

28. Mount Everest is located in what mountain range?
a) Andes
b) Alps
c) Himalayas

29. Sweden's longest land border is with what other country?

30. In terms of area, what is the largest desert in Africa?

31. What is the capital of Sweden?

32. What is the capital of Brazil?

AaBbCcDdEe

33. The country of Estonia is located on which continent?

34. What is the capital of Italy?
   a) Rome
   b) Milan
   c) Naples

35. The island of Hispaniola in the Caribbean is divided between two nations. The Dominican Republic is one of them. What is the other?

AaBbCcDdEe

7x7=49

36. In 1787, what was the first state to ratify the Constitution and join the U.S.?

37. During what decade did James Marshall discover gold nuggets, sparking the famous California Gold Rush?

38. On March 14, 1794, who received a patent for the cotton gin?

39. Which of the following Native American groups was a Great Plains tribe?
a) Cherokee
b) Tlingit
c) Sioux

40. Name this Florida city, settled by the Spanish in 1565, which is known today as America's oldest city.

41. The international organization known as the Red Cross started in 1863. Who is best known for founding its American branch in 1881?

Brain Bubble

A Nobel Cause

From its modest beginnings, the Red Cross has grown today into an organization with 180 national members and more than 1.5 million volunteers. It uses these resources to provide help to the needy in times of both war and peace. Since it was founded, the organization has received three Nobel Peace Prizes in recognition of its efforts.

42. In the 1800s, people called abolitionists worked to abolish what practice in the United States?

43. What was the name of the period of rebuilding and repair that followed the U.S. Civil War?

44. The period of U.S. history known as the Great Depression occurred primarily in which decade?

45. Japanese forces bombed what U.S. military base on December 7, 1941?

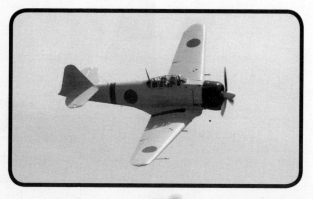

WORLD HISTORY

46. Ivan the Terrible was a czar of what country?

47. Puerto Rico was a colony of what country immediately before the U.S. gained possession of it in 1898?

48. This pilot was the first woman to make a solo flight in an airplane across the Atlantic Ocean.
What was her name?

Brain Benders

49. Who was the first U.S. Secretary of State?

50. Spanish explorer Juan Ponce de León was searching for what mythical spring when he visited the area that is now Florida in the 1500s?

SOCIAL STUDIES

1. **The U.S. Vice President**. The Vice President casts his or her vote to break a tie vote in the Senate.

2. **Six years**. Senators are elected to these terms by popular vote.

3. **25 years old**. Several people in their mid to late 20s have been elected to Congress.

4. **True**. Even the children of illegal immigrants are considered to be U.S. citizens, although there have been suggestions to change this tradition.

5. **The right to vote**. Prior to this amendment, most states restricted women's voting rights or denied them entirely.

6. **Abraham Lincoln**. The image sits between two columns of the Lincoln Memorial, also pictured on the coin.

U.S PRESIDENTS

7. **January 20**. The swearing-in ceremony takes place at noon.

8. **10 years**. A president can be elected only to two four-year terms, but can serve longer under unusual conditions.

9. **Andrew Johnson**. The impeachment occurred in 1868.

10. **1860**. He served until his death by assassination in 1865.

11. **James**. Six presidents — Madison, Monroe, Polk, Buchanan, Garfield, and (Jimmy) Carter — bore this first name.

12. **Zachary**. He served as President from 1849 to 1850.

13. **Woodrow Wilson**. On April 2, Wilson asked Congress to declare war on Germany. The official statement was issued four days later.

14. **Herbert Hoover**. He served from 1929 to 1933.

15. **Missouri**. Truman served in this position from 1934 to 1944.

16. **Rutherford Birchard Hayes**. His term ran from 1877 through 1881.

17. **George Washington**. Now maintained as a tourist site, the home is located near Alexandria, Virginia.

U.S. GEOGRAPHY

18. **The Missouri River**. This river is 2,450 miles from end to end.

19. **Minnesota**. The Mississippi starts here and ends 2,340 miles later at the Gulf of Mexico.

20. **a. Puerto Rico**. Bermuda is associated with the United Kingdom. Aruba is a territory of the Netherlands.

21. **49**. Hawaii is the only state south of this imaginary line.

22. **Three**. The states are Ohio, Oklahoma, and Oregon.

23. **Hawaii**. This island state is more southerly than any point on the continental U.S.

24. **Arizona**. The Grand Canyon lies in the northwestern part of the state.

WORLD GEOGRAPHY

25. **Switzerland**.

26. **Africa**. This inactive volcano is located in northeastern Tanzania.

27. **Portugal**. This nation makes up most of the western edge of the Iberian Peninsula.

28. **c. Himalayas**. With an elevation of 29,035 feet, Mount Everest is the tallest mountain in the Himalayas or anywhere else on Earth.

29. **Norway**. Sweden also shares a much shorter border with Finland.

30. **The Sahara Desert**. It is almost as large as the continental U.S.

31. **Stockholm**. The capital has been Sweden's most important city for at least 800 years.

32. **Brasilia**. The city was specially built in 1960 to become Brazil's capital.

33. **Europe**. Estonia is bordered by Russia and Latvia.

34. **a. Rome**. It is Italy's largest and most populous city.

35. **Haiti**. This nation occupies the western third of the island.

U.S. HISTORY

36. **Delaware**. The state took this historic action on December 7.

37. **The 1840s**. Marshall discovered gold in California's American River on January 24, 1848.

38. **Eli Whitney**. His invention was a mechanical device that removed seeds from cotton.

39. **c. Sioux**. The Cherokees were a Southeastern tribe. The Tlingits were a Northwestern tribe.

40. **St. Augustine**. The city is the home of America's oldest masonry fort.

41. **Nurse Clara Barton**.

42. **Slavery**. The abolitionist movement reached its strongest point between 1830 and 1861, when the U.S. Civil War began.

43. **Reconstruction**. This period lasted from 1865 to 1877.

44. **The 1930s**. Historians agree that this period started in 1929 and continued until about 1940.

45. **Pearl Harbor**. This base was located near Honolulu, Hawaii. The surprise attack led the U.S. to declare war on Japan on December 8, 1941.

WORLD HISTORY

46. **Russia**. Ivan ruled this nation in the late 1500s.

47. **Spain**. Today, Puerto Rico is an unincorporated U.S. territory.

48. **Amelia Earhart**. She made her historic flight on May 20, 1932.

BRAIN BENDERS

49. **Thomas Jefferson**. Before becoming the third U.S. President, he served in this position from 1789 to 1793.

50. **The Fountain of Youth**. According to legend, the waters of this spring had the ability to restore youth.

Did you
☐ pass or
☐ fail?

5TH Grade

You've reached the make-it-or-break-it level:
the fifth grade! It's time for your final exam.
Will you be smarter than the classroom students
on TV? Or, like those grown-up students
stumped by the toughest questions,
will you fail to make the grade?

1. How many people signed the U.S. Declaration of Independence?

2. In the United States, people elect representatives to run the country. This form of government is known as what?
a) Monarchy
b) Republic
c) Dictatorship

3. Which of these powers belongs to the national government of the U.S.?
a) Set up public schools
b) Print and coin money
c) Conduct elections

4. **True or False?** A state's number of Congressional Representatives depends on its population.

5. The U.S. Census is the official count taken of the population in the United States. How often is the count done?

Brain Bubble

More Than a Number

The U.S. Census does more than count our nation's population. It also collects information about each person's age, race, job, income, lifestyle, and many other topics. The government uses this information to outline voting districts in each state as well as to plan highways, schools, hospitals, parks, and other public necessities.

7x7=49

U.S. PRESIDENTS

6. What former U.S. President was the first American to win the Nobel Peace Prize?

7. Who immediately followed Abraham Lincoln as President of the United States?

8. Who was the only person to be elected U.S. President four times?

9. Who was the fourth President of the United States?

10. What former U.S. President created the framework for "The Virginia Plan" that structured our government into three branches?

AaBbCcDdEe

11. In 1823, what document written by the U.S. President stated that America was against "future colonization by any European Powers"?

12. Thomas Jefferson died on July 4, 1826. What other U.S. President died on the very same day?

13. The U.S. President has the power to reject bills that are passed by Congress. What is this action called?

14. Published in the 1780s, the Federalist Papers were written by Alexander Hamilton, John Jay, and what man who would later be a U.S. President?

15. Who was the youngest person to become President of the United States?

AaBbcDdEe

7x7=49

16. Who was the only U.S. President who was never married?

17. The Gettysburg Address, given by former U.S. President Abraham Lincoln, begins with what famous 6 words?

Brain Bubble
Memorable Words

President Abraham Lincoln delivered the Gettysburg Address during the dedication of a cemetery for fallen Civil War heroes. In his speech, Lincoln talked about the ideals on which America was founded. He asked people to remember the reasons for the Civil War and to fight even harder to preserve the traditional American way of life. A brief three minutes in length, the Gettysburg Address is considered one of the most inspiring speeches ever given by an American leader.

U.S. GEOGRAPHY

18. **True or False?** Ohio shares a border with Illinois.

19. Completed in 1825, what man-made waterway in New York State connects the Hudson River to the Great Lakes?

20. Which of the Great Lakes lies farthest east?

21. **True or False?** The states of Alaska and Texas are roughly the same size.

22. The Aleutian Islands are part of what state?

WORLD GEOGRAPHY

23. The Strait of Magellan runs through the southern tip of which continent?

24. The Gobi Desert is located on which continent?

25. Russia's longest land border is with what other country?

26. In terms of distance, the U.S. is closest to which of the following countries?
a) Cuba
b) Brazil
c) Russia

27. The island region known as Micronesia is located in which ocean?

U.S. HISTORY

28. What Revolutionary leader wrote the influential pamphlet "Common Sense" in 1776?

29. During the U.S. Civil War, what city in Virginia was the capital of the Confederacy?

30. What was the real first name of U.S. Civil War General "Stonewall" Jackson?

31. Who was the first Chief Justice of the U.S. Supreme Court?

32. What Revolutionary leader famously uttered the words, "Give me liberty or give me death!" in a speech at the second Virginia Convention?

33. What U.S. Revolutionary War hero is credited with saying, "I have not yet begun to fight"?

34. In the late 1700s, the U.S. opened an area called the Northwest Territory to exploration and settlement. This area did *not* include which present-day state?
a) Indiana
b) Wisconsin
c) Missouri

35. In 1803, the U.S. agreed to buy the area that makes up the present-day U.S. Midwest from France. What was this transaction called?

36. Prospectors who participated in the California Gold Rush were known by what nickname?
a) Twenty-sixers
b) Thirty-eighters
c) Forty-niners

37. True or False? The "Underground Railroad" was a nickname given to the first U.S. subway system, built in the late 1800s in Boston, Massachusetts.

38. In the U.S. Civil War, what color were the uniforms of Northern soldiers?

WORLD HISTORY

39. What Egyptian queen was the wife of Roman General Mark Antony?

40. The ancient region known as Mesopotamia was bordered by the Euphrates and what other river?

41. The League of Nations was formed at the conclusion of what war?

42. Which Frenchman was the first European explorer to navigate the St. Lawrence River in Canada?

43. Charles Lindbergh flew the first solo nonstop transatlantic flight from New York to what city?

44. The Hundred Years' War of the 14th and 15th centuries was primarily a conflict between England and what other country?

45. Copernicus, the legendary 16th century astronomer, was born in what country?

46. In 1961, a concrete barrier was built all the way around the German city of West Berlin. What was the name of this barrier?

AaBbccDdEe

7x7=49

Brain Benders

47. How many U.S. Presidents have resigned from office?

48. What American pilot was the first person to exceed the speed of sound in an airplane?

77

SOCIAL STUDIES

1. **56**. The document was signed by all of the delegates to the U.S. Congress.

2. **b. Republic**. A republic is one type of democratic government.

3. **b. Print and coin money**. State governments are responsible for public schools and elections.

4. **True**. The bigger the population, the more representatives a state is permitted to elect.

5. **Every 10 years**. The U.S. Census is conducted in years that end in "0" (1980, 1990, 2000, etc.).

U.S. PRESIDENTS

6. **Theodore Roosevelt**. He received his award in 1906.

7. **Andrew Johnson**. He became President after Lincoln's assassination in 1865.

8. **Franklin Delano Roosevelt**. Today, the rules have been changed so that U.S. Presidents cannot be elected more than twice.

9. **James Madison**. His term ran from 1809 to 1817.

10. **James Madison**. He drafted the plan, which was devised by a team of Virginia delegates.

11. **The Monroe Doctrine**. This document was penned by President James Monroe.

12. **John Adams**. He was 90 years old when he died.

13. **A veto**. Vetoed bills can still become laws if Congress passes them a second time by a certain majority.

14. **James Madison**. He wrote 29 of the 85 articles included in this collection.

15. **Theodore Roosevelt**. He was 42 years old when he assumed the presidency in 1901.

16. **James Buchanan**. His fiancée broke off the engagement.

17. "**Four score and seven years ago**." Lincoln gave this speech on November 19, 1863, in Gettysburg, Pennsylvania.

U.S. GEOGRAPHY

18. **False**. The state of Indiana separates Ohio and Illinois.

19. **The Erie Canal**. Construction on this waterway began in 1817.

20. **Lake Ontario**. This lake makes up part of the New York/Ontario border.

21. **False**. Alaska is more than double the size of Texas.

22. **Alaska**. This chain curves west from the tip of the Alaskan Peninsula.

WORLD GEOGRAPHY

23. **South America**. This waterway crosses Chile and is a passage between the Atlantic and Pacific oceans.

24. **Asia**. The Gobi covers parts of China and Mongolia.

25. **Kazakhstan**. This former Soviet state borders southwestern Russia.

26. **c. Russia**. The Alaskan and Russian mainlands are only about 55 miles apart at their closest point. They are separated by the Bering Strait.

27. **The Pacific Ocean**. Micronesia includes over 2,000 islands and is located east of the Philippines.

U.S. HISTORY

28. **Thomas Paine**. This widely read pamphlet called for U.S. independence from Britain.

29. **Richmond, Virginia**. The city was appointed the Confederate capital soon after Virginia seceded from the U.S. on April 17, 1861.

30. **Thomas**. He earned the nickname "Stonewall" during an early U.S. Civil War battle.

31. **John Jay**. He served from 1789 to 1795.

32. **Patrick Henry**. He gave his famous speech on March 23, 1775.

33. **John Paul Jones**. He said these words during a 1779 sea battle.

34. **c. Missouri**. The Northwest Territory included all of present-day Ohio, Indiana, Illinois, Michigan, Wisconsin, and parts of Minnesota.

35. **The Louisiana Purchase**. This purchase nearly doubled the size of the United States.

36. **c. Forty-niners**. They got this nickname because they arrived in the year 1849.

37. **False**. The Underground Railroad was a system of escape routes for slaves that operated in the U.S. in the early- to mid-1800s.

38. **Blue**. Southern soldiers mostly wore gray uniforms.

WORLD HISTORY

39. **Cleopatra**. She married Mark Antony in 37 BCE.

40. **The Tigris River**. It flows from the mountains of Turkey through Iraq.

41. **World War One**. The League's purpose, which ultimately failed, was to prevent future world wars.

42. **Jacques Cartier**. He made his historic voyage from 1535 to 1536.

43. **Paris**. Lindbergh made this flight from May 20-21, 1927.

44. **France**. This war was fought over the French throne, to which both France and England laid claim.

45. **Poland**. Copernicus was born on February 19, 1473, in the Polish city of Torun.

46. **The Berlin Wall**. It was built to separate the people of Western-allied Germany from the Eastern-allied parts of the country.

BRAIN BENDERS

47. **One**. Richard Nixon resigned his position on August 9, 1974, in the midst of a scandal.

48. **Chuck Yeager**. He achieved this goal in 1947, when he was 24 years old.

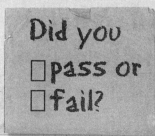

Did you
☐ pass or
☐ fail?

GRADUATION TIME

How did you do? Even if you didn't get every question right, real life isn't like the TV show. You don't flunk out because of a wrong answer. You get the chance to try again — and trying again is how you learn.

Go back to any questions that gave you trouble. Study the correct answers until you know them by heart. Before long, you'll be a history expert. More important, you'll be able to say the line that many adults haven't been able to say in Mr. Foxworthy's TV classroom:

"Yes, I AM smarter than a 5th grader!"